Philosophy or Religion

Are We Truly Walking a Path of Awakening?

ButterflyMan

This book is a work of philosophical analysis and interpretation.
It does not promote or oppose any religion, belief system, or
ideology.

Printed in the United States of America
First Edition
ISBN: 979-8-90217-022-8

Directory

Preface: "Philosophy, or religion?"

I didn't write this book to create a new belief.

I wrote it to **question belief itself**.

The Buddha was never meant to be a god.
He was a philosopher—the summit of human wisdom.
He taught impermanence, suffering, and egolessness.
He dismantled illusion and offered insight.
He did not demand temples, incense, chanting, or statues.

And yet, what did we do?

We turned his wisdom into a **religion**,
then turned that religion into a **business**.

"Buy merit."
"Release fish."
"Donate gold."
None of this is awakening. It is anesthesia.
We no longer **live the Buddha's truth**, we **buy blessings**.

I've never liked temples where "virtue is sold."
I prefer to sit quietly with the Buddha's silence and gaze.
Then one day, after reading Western philosophy—
Schopenhauer, Spinoza, Kant, Nietzsche—
I **felt the connection**.
They were all echoing the Buddha, in different words.

I discovered I was not the first to compare them.
But perhaps I could be the first to **publicly say what others dare not**:

> The Buddha is **not religion**.
> The Buddha is **pure philosophy**.
> Not to be worshipped—but to be **lived**.

This is not just a philosophical argument.
It is a necessary awakening for the future of China.

If Chinese people remain in temples praying for mercy, they will never become owners of their destiny.
Awakening is not praying.
It is **claiming your equal rights**,
to be the true owners of the land, the wealth, the system.

Buddha never taught obedience.
He taught **awakening**.

This book is a spark.
Not for worship—but for awakening.
Not for faith—but for freedom.

The Origins of Wisdom: The Misinterpretation and Evolution of Eastern and Western Philosophies

Introduction: Philosophy or Religion?

Philosophy is the beginning of liberation; religion, often, is the tool of control.

In the East, philosophy was religiously sanctified, deified, and eventually absorbed by centralized power.
In the West, while more formally free, philosophy too was often constrained—by economy, politics, and pragmatism.

This book seeks to trace back to the origin of true wisdom—beyond superstition, beyond ritual—to revive a world guided by insight, not blind worship.

Chapter 1: Buddha — A Philosopher, Not a God

- The Buddha's original teachings—Four Noble Truths, the Noble Eightfold Path—were not religious commandments but rational life wisdom.
- He rejected gods and absolutes, focusing instead on inner observation and awakening.
- Yet over time, Buddhism was transformed—especially in India and China—into a religion full of deities and rituals.
- Who misunderstood the Buddha? And who preserved his wisdom?

Chapter 2: Zen and the Japanese Exception

- Why did Japan preserve the *philosophical* nature of Buddhism while others sanctified it?
- Zen Buddhism emphasized experience, awareness, and simplicity—anchoring wisdom into daily life.
- The fusion of Bushido and Zen shaped a rational modern consciousness.
- The Meiji Restoration drew strength from this philosophical clarity, accepting modernization without losing cultural identity.

Chapter 3: The Corruption of Buddhism — Superstition, Commerce, and Inner Insurance

- Across China and Southeast Asia, Buddhism morphed into an offering-based superstition.
- Temples became wish-granting centers; incense burned for luck, not enlightenment.
- Religion became a psychological lottery ticket—false hope sold as comfort.
- True wisdom was buried beneath rituals, donations, and divine promises.

Chapter 4: Schopenhauer, Spinoza, Kant — Silent Heirs of the Buddha

- Schopenhauer deeply studied and admired the Buddha, bringing Eastern insight into Western pessimism and will theory.
- Spinoza's monism echoes the Buddhist idea of oneness and non-self.
- Kant's categorical imperative reflects the Buddha's middle path and inner moral compass.
- These Western thinkers inherited the Buddha's wisdom—without ever calling it "Buddhism."

Chapter 5: Zhuangzi and Nietzsche — Twin Dissidents of East and West

- Zhuangzi: a destroyer of systems, language, and power structures—radical individual freedom.
- Nietzsche: a Western Zhuangzi—questioning values, unmasking power, embracing the void.
- Both offered existential freedom beyond authority and conformity.
- Nietzsche rephrased Zhuangzi's detachment into a Western dialectic of will and nihilism.

Chapter 6: Freud and the Daoist Unconscious

- Freud's psychoanalysis—id, ego, and superego—echo Daoist thought on natural instincts and harmony.
- Daoist *wu wei* (non-action) parallels the therapeutic uncovering of repressed impulses.
- "Knowing stillness" and "returning to origin" prefigure the idea of unconscious drives.
- Freud's method might be seen as modern "Zen therapy."

Chapter 7: Why the East Lost Philosophy

- In the Warring States period, hundreds of schools contended—philosophy flourished.
- But with the rise of Han Confucian orthodoxy, thought was centralized, and diversity crushed.
- Worship replaced questioning. Authority replaced dialogue.
- By the Qing Dynasty, the East had no more philosophers—only scholars and servants.

Chapter 8: The Buddha and Marx — Strange Allies?

- The Buddha's ideal of a just, desireless society shares echoes with Marx's vision.
- "From each according to ability, to each according to need" resonates with Buddhist communalism.
- Yet Marx was materialist; Buddha spiritual.
- Lenin, not the Buddha, turned Marxism into a political weapon—wisdom became firebrand ideology.

Chapter 12: Philosophy Hijacked by Politics

- Why are philosophers feared by kings and praised by tyrants—only after they're dead?
- From church dogma to Communist Party doctrine, thinking has always been dangerous.
- Philosophy often becomes a decoration for power.
- Real philosophy must be de-sanctified, reclaimed by the people, and rooted in human dignity.

Chapter 13: Reclaiming Wisdom — Beyond Worship, Into Awareness

- Awakening begins not with belief, but with doubt.
- Education must be philosophized; daily life must return to awareness.
- Zen is not meditation—it's piercing through illusion.
- Future humanity needs both Eastern insight and Western analysis—united as "rational spirituality."

📘 Conclusion: Wisdom is the Highest Compassion

- Philosophy is not cold logic—it is compassion in its deepest form.
- The Buddha did not seek to be worshipped, but to help others wake up.
- In an age of collapse—economic, political, spiritual—philosophy must return as a guiding light.
- This book is an invitation: to think, to question, to live freely—not to believe, but to awaken.

Afterword — When Worship Ends, Awakening Begins

The age of blind belief is ending. The age of conscious humanity is beginning. Let us meet not in temples, but in truth.

📎 Appendices

- **A. Comparative Table**: Buddha vs. Schopenhauer / Spinoza / Kant
- **B. Quote Atlas**: Zhuangzi vs. Nietzsche side-by-side passages
- **C. Timeline**: Zen Buddhism and Japan's intellectual modernization
- **D. Essential Readings**: Original and secondary texts on Buddha, Zhuangzi, Nietzsche, Freud, etc.
- **E. Map of Philosophical Evolution**: Religion → Philosophy → Politics across civilizations

Chapter 1: The Buddha – The Misunderstood Philosopher

Not a Deity, but an Awakener

I. We Have Missed the Buddha

Who is the Buddha as we know him?

Is he the golden statue enshrined in temples, seated in eternal calm?
Is he the object of incense smoke and prayers for fortune and safety?
Or is he the kind-faced sage chanting "Amitabha" in dramas and folktales?

Few realize that all of these representations **deeply distort the original intention of the Buddha**.
He was not a god-maker, but a god-breaker.
Not a preacher of faith, but a thinker of freedom.
Not the founder of religion, but a philosopher who sought to transcend religion through **wisdom and awakening**.

In his earliest teachings, there is no creator, no divine judgment, no miracles.
What he offers is a path of inquiry—a rational and experiential analysis of suffering and liberation.
His path is a form of **existential philosophy**, a guide toward inner clarity and freedom.

II. What the Buddha Taught Was Philosophy, Not Religion

In the earliest Pali texts—*Digha Nikaya, Majjhima Nikaya, Samyutta Nikaya*—we find this crucial distinction:

The Buddha never said: "Believe in me."
He said: "Come and see. Observe and verify for yourself."

This is entirely different from faith-based religion, where belief precedes understanding.

The Buddha's path is built on **empirical observation, self-discipline, and rational inquiry**.
He taught the Four Noble Truths and the Noble Eightfold Path; he emphasized impermanence (*anicca*), non-self (*anatta*), and dependent origination (*paticcasamuppada*).

These are not divine commandments—they are **philosophical statements** on human existence, suffering, and consciousness.

The Buddha never intended to found a "religion."
He sought to awaken minds, not gather followers.
He asked for insight, not worship.

Early Buddhism was **a philosophy**, not a religion.
It was a profound Eastern form of existential inquiry.

III. The Fate of Philosophy: Wisdom Turned into Religion

So why is the Buddha now seen and treated as a god?

Because as history unfolded, **philosophy was consumed by faith, power, and ritual**.

From Emperor Ashoka's reign onward, Buddhism expanded rapidly—politically and institutionally.
To appeal to mass psychology and political needs, the Buddha was deified; sutras became mystical texts; practice became ceremony.

When Buddhism entered China, it merged with Taoist cosmology and Confucian social hierarchy.
The result was a transformation:

- Guanyin became a wish-granting deity.
- Kṣitigarbha became a judge of hell.
- Amitabha offered paradise in the afterlife.

Thus, the Buddha's original vision—**self-inquiry, self-liberation, self-awareness**—
was buried under **rituals, incense, fortune-seeking, and superstition**.

Philosophy became theology.
Wisdom became worship.
Awakening became escapism.

IV. Why Japan Preserved the Buddha as a Philosopher

An important exception to this religious distortion is Japan.

While early Japanese Buddhism also carried ritualistic elements, the rise of **Zen Buddhism** preserved the **philosophical essence** of the Buddha's teaching.

Zen does not speak of heaven or hell.
Zen does not promote saviors or divine promises.
Instead, Zen emphasizes:

- "Not relying on words or scriptures."
- "Direct pointing to the mind."
- "Seeing one's true nature and becoming Buddha."

It values:

- Direct experience over doctrine.
- Stillness and mindfulness over belief.
- The present moment over distant heavens.

This allowed Zen to integrate with **Bushido (the way of the warrior), Japanese aesthetics, craftsmanship,**

and daily life, forming a **philosophy of being**, not merely a religion.

Zen is not a retreat—it is insight.
Zen is not mysticism—it is lucidity.

V. The Spirit of Awakening: Striking Parallels in Western Philosophy

Looking across civilizations, we find surprising resonances between the Buddha and Western thinkers:

- **Schopenhauer** saw suffering as rooted in desire and was directly influenced by the Upanishads and Buddhist texts.
- **Spinoza** taught that "God is Nature," and that the self is part of a unified whole—similar to *anatta* and *interdependence*.
- **Kant** emphasized reason and moral duty, where freedom means obeying the moral law within—mirroring the Buddha's ethical path.
- **Nietzsche**, though critical of religion, called for self-overcoming and personal revaluation of values—echoing Buddhist liberation from illusion.

These thinkers never claimed to be Buddhists,
yet they inherited the Buddha's **philosophical essence**:

> **To trace the roots of suffering, to transcend desire, and to reclaim the clarity of the self.**

VI. Philosophy Is Compassion, Not Cold Logic

Many today see philosophy as abstract, lifeless, even arrogant.
But the Buddha showed otherwise:

> True philosophy is the highest form of compassion.

It responds not to theories, but to suffering.
It does not evade reality—it confronts and liberates it.

The Buddha's wisdom is not theoretical—it is practical.
Not verbal—not divine—but experiential.

He never asked us to believe in him.
He asked us to awaken within ourselves.

VII. How Do We Return to the Buddha of Philosophy?

The Buddha never asked to be worshipped.
He asked us to awaken.

- He was not a god, but a guide.
- Not a savior, but a mirror.
- Not a voice to obey, but a path to walk.

To understand the Buddha is not to light incense.
It is to light our inner clarity.

As he once said:

> **"Do not look outside for refuge. Your own mind is the lamp."**

Chapter 2: The Zen Miracle

How Japan Preserved Buddhism as Philosophy

I. What Would Buddhism Have Become Without Zen?

In the centuries after the Buddha's passing, the seeds of his philosophy spread across regions—and met very different fates.

In India, Buddhism was eventually marginalized by Brahmanism (later Hinduism), and nearly disappeared.
In China, Buddhism flourished, but was deeply entangled with Daoist cosmology and Confucian hierarchy, becoming **temple-based, deity-driven, and utilitarian**.
In Southeast Asia, it evolved into a communal religion rooted in karma and reincarnation.

Only in Japan did Buddhism resist full religious and political assimilation—and instead became **philosophical, aesthetic, and integrated into daily life**.

At the heart of this transformation was **Zen**.

> Zen is not religion. Zen is not theory. Zen is the transformation of philosophy into a lived experiment of awareness.

II. "No Reliance on Words": A Radical Anti-Theological Philosophy

Zen, introduced to China by Bodhidharma, made a bold declaration:

> "No reliance on words or letters.

A separate transmission outside the scriptures.
Directly pointing to the human mind.
Seeing one's true nature and becoming Buddha."

This meant:

- No dependency on texts, but reliance on direct experience.
- No focus on rituals, but on inner realization.
- No worship of external powers, but awakening from within.

In a religious culture dominated by scripture, ceremony, and institutional authority, this was radical—even heretical.

But it was exactly this stance that **preserved the philosophical core of Buddhism**.
Zen didn't reject texts—it rejected the **lazy thinking** that confuses words with insight.

> In Zen, even if you memorize the sutras, if you don't see your mind clearly, you haven't understood the Buddha.

III. How Zen Became a Way of Life in Japan

Zen entered Japan during the Kamakura period—a time of upheaval and war.
The rising samurai class sought spiritual strength that was simple, direct, and inner-focused.

Zen matched their need for calm in chaos, focus in uncertainty.

Core elements of Zen:

Practice	Form	Inner Meaning
Zazen (seated meditation)	Silent sitting, breath awareness	Presence, clearing mental noise
No-Form	Non-attachment to rituals or doctrines	Dissolution of ego and craving
Mind Is Buddha	No external deity; Buddha is within	Enlightenment as self-realization
Everyday Practice	Walking, eating, working, living	Daily life as path to awakening

This philosophy took root across Japanese culture:

- **Bushido**: Calm in battle, dignity in death, non-attachment to fear
- **Tea Ceremony**: Mindfulness and presence through ritual simplicity
- **Ikebana (Flower Arrangement)**: Contemplation of emptiness, impermanence, and form
- **Architecture and Gardens**: Minimalism as expression of inner clarity

Zen ceased to be "religion."
It became **Japan's foundational philosophy**—an invisible structure beneath its art, ethics, and education.

IV. How Zen Supported Japan's Leap into Modern Civilization

By the late 19th century, Japan faced existential crisis under pressure from Western imperialism.

During the Meiji Restoration, Japan adopted Western technology, governance, and institutions.
But—**unlike China—it didn't completely reject its cultural heritage**.
Zen, unlike Confucianism, carried no heavy baggage of feudal hierarchy or dogma.
It offered a **non-religious spiritual framework** that supported personal discipline and adaptability.

Zen's compatibility with modern values:

Western Modern Concept	**Zen Parallel**
Subjectivity	Everyone can awaken by seeing their mind
Free Will	Liberation through non-attachment to desire
Rational Inquiry	No blind faith—truth must be verified through experience
Anti-Authoritarianism	"If you see the Buddha, kill the Buddha"
Aesthetic Minimalism	Wabi-sabi: beauty in imperfection, impermanence

In this way, Zen helped Japan build **a modern state with spiritual stability**, allowing rapid industrialization without total cultural dislocation.

V. Why the West Became Obsessed with Zen

In the 20th century, Zen—through D.T. Suzuki and others—was introduced to the West and quickly captivated philosophers, psychologists, and artists.

- **Martin Heidegger** saw echoes of existential "Being" in Zen thought

- **Alan Watts** interpreted Zen as a remedy for modern alienation
- **Artists like John Cage, Akira Kurosawa, and Stanley Kubrick** found inspiration in Zen aesthetics
- **Post-Freudians** saw Zen's "emptiness" as a profound response to the unconscious

Why did Zen resonate so deeply?

Because:

- Zen doesn't demand belief
- Zen doesn't dictate metaphysics
- Zen doesn't promise salvation

Zen is **practice, perception, presence**.

In a world plagued by anxiety, disconnection, and post-religious confusion, Zen became a **language of inner clarity**—free from ideology.

VI. The New Danger: Zen as Fashion, Not Philosophy

But today, even Zen faces distortion.

- Meditation becomes a productivity hack.
- "Zen" becomes interior design.
- Apps sell "calm" as commodity.

The real Zen—

- Doesn't comfort you.
- Doesn't decorate your life.
- **It challenges you to see through illusion, ego, and escapism.**

The future of Zen depends on whether we **recognize its philosophical blade**, or merely polish its surface for peace of mind.

VII. Conclusion: Zen Is a Mirror, Not a Mask

Zen is a miracle because it:

1. **Preserved the Buddha's non-theistic, self-liberating core**
2. **Escaped the religious trap of idolatry and hierarchy**
3. **Became a bridge between tradition and modern consciousness**

Zen is not an answer—it is a method.
Not faith—but awareness.
Not a retreat—but a confrontation with the real.

As the Zen saying goes:

"To see one's nature is to see Buddha."

Chapter 3: The Corruption of Buddhism

When Wisdom Becomes Comfort and Commodity

I. From a Path of Awakening to a "Comfort Zone"

Once upon a time, Buddhism was a path toward awakening, liberation, and inner freedom.

But today, in many societies, it has turned into something quite different:

- A **psychological sedative**,
- A **ritualized talisman**,
- Even a **lifestyle brand**.

More and more people are drawn to Buddhism not to contemplate **the nature of life and death**,
but simply because they feel "too stressed," "can't sleep," or "need to calm down."

So now, Zen meditation is marketed as **stress relief**,
chanting is offered as a **self-soothing tool**,
incense is lit for **spiritual ambience**,
and Buddha statues are used as **interior decor**.

What was once a practice of awakening has been reduced to a pursuit of comfort.

On the surface, this looks like Buddhism becoming "popular" or "accessible,"
but in truth, it's a case of the Buddha's philosophy being **instrumentalized and distorted**.

II. When the Buddha Becomes a Therapist or a Wish-Granting Machine

To the modern urban individual, Buddhism increasingly plays the following roles:

- A **mood regulator**: visit a temple when overwhelmed, meditate for calm, listen to a mindfulness podcast;
- A **wish-granting system**: for success, love, wealth, or health—light incense, draw fortune slips, make an offering;
- A **psychological refuge**: when relationships fail or work becomes unbearable, Buddhism offers a "safe space."

The Buddha once urged us to face the **nature of suffering**.
Now he's used to **distract us from suffering**.

He taught us to **let go of desire**.
Now he's invoked to **help us fulfill desire**.

Buddhism has shifted from being **a path of insight** to **a tool of utility**.

This is not just a misreading of the Buddha.
It's a symptom of a broader modern condition:

People no longer seek truth—they seek relief.
They no longer face problems—they want escape.

III. The Commercialization of the Mind — Buddhism Under Capitalism

Modern consumer society excels at turning everything into a product.

Buddhism is no exception.

- **Temples as businesses**: tiered incense, donation boards, premium blessings, "gold-plated" statues;
- **Internet monks**: livestreaming karma talks, selling prayer beads, recruiting online disciples;
- **"Buddha lifestyle"**: a subculture among young professionals seeking "detachment," "peace," or "Zen dating";
- **Merchandise**: meditation mats, aroma diffusers, mala bracelets, Zen-style fashion, minimalist furniture.

Buddhism, once an inward journey, has become an **external aesthetic**.
Wisdom, once earned through discipline, is now **branded and sold**.

> Awakening has become a lifestyle.
> Enlightenment has become a slogan.
>
> This is more than dilution—this is corruption.

Buddhism no longer asks "Are you awakening?" It asks, "Are you emotionally soothed?"

IV. Why Do People Crave This "Gentle and Harmless Buddhism"?

Let's not judge too quickly.

Modern people live under relentless pressure—
loneliness, anxiety, performance, comparison, burnout.
They crave something **gentle, non-judgmental, and comforting—**
a spiritual "weighted blanket."

And Buddhism—especially Buddhism stripped of its philosophical rigor—
perfectly fits this psychological need.

- It doesn't preach original sin or hellfire.
- It doesn't demand obedience or repentance.
- It doesn't intimidate with theology or complexity.

Words like **"compassion," "stillness," "letting go"**—
once embedded in serious discipline—
now become soft and marketable.

But here is the question:

Is this nourishment? Or is it sedation?
Is it healing? Or is it avoidance?

V. The Buddha Never Wanted Us to Be "Comfortable"

Look back at the Buddha's life:

- He renounced a kingdom—not to escape stress, but to investigate **the source of human suffering**.

- He practiced harsh asceticism—not for relaxation, but to probe the **limits of desire and the body**.

- He attained enlightenment—not through feel-good meditation, but by **seeing through the illusion of self**.

The Buddha never promised comfort.
He sought **clarity**.

He was not a therapist, not a motivational speaker, not a life coach.

> He was a radical thinker of **existence itself**.
> His goal wasn't "stress reduction"—it was **awakening**.
> Not a comfort zone, but **a gateway to truth**.

VI. How Can We Reapproach Buddhism Today?

To reclaim the philosophical core of Buddhism, we must ask ourselves three questions:

1. **Why do I approach Buddhism?** To escape reality, or to see it clearly?

2. **What am I practicing?** Temporary calm, or sustained awareness?

3. **Who is the Buddha to me?** A kindly protector, or a fearless challenger of illusion?

We must shift from being **spiritual consumers** to **practitioners of wisdom**.

Not just “watching a Dharma talk” or “buying a bracelet,”
but deeply engaging in reading, thinking, observing, and living—even if only through a single honest moment of self-confrontation.

VII. Conclusion: Escaping the Trap of Soft Illusions

The corruption of Buddhism does not mean it has lost its value.

On the contrary—it reminds us that the **path of wisdom is never easy**, nor should it be.

If we reduce Buddhism to a comfort drug or cultural accessory,
we abandon its most precious gift:

The courage to face pain,
The clarity to see through illusion,
And the strength to transcend the self.

The Buddha is not in the temple.
Not in the rituals.
Not even in the scriptures.

He is found in the moment we stop escaping,
stop pretending,
and finally choose to **wake up**.

Chapter 4: Schopenhauer, Spinoza, and Kant

How Western Philosophers Inherited the Buddha's Wisdom

I. The Silent Dialogue Between East and West

When we speak of "the wisdom of the Buddha," we often imagine it as something exotic, spiritual, and exclusively Eastern—
a world away from Western philosophy.

But this assumption collapses upon closer examination.

Beginning in the 17th and especially the 19th century, many of the **greatest Western philosophers**, though rooted in completely different languages, cultures, and religious traditions,
began to **echo the insights of the Buddha**—
not by imitation, but through independent inquiry into **the same timeless questions**:

- Where does human suffering come from?
- What is the nature of desire?
- Is the "self" real or an illusion?
- Can morality and freedom arise from within, not from above?
- How do we awaken from delusion and live with clarity?

These are precisely the questions the Buddha sat under the Bodhi tree to contemplate, 2,500 years ago.

II. Schopenhauer: The First Western Philosopher to Grasp the Buddha

If one Western philosopher can be said to have **genuinely understood** the Buddha, it is **Arthur Schopenhauer**.

Often labeled the "father of philosophical pessimism," Schopenhauer was, in many ways,
a modern interpreter of the Buddha's existential insight.

Core Parallels:

Buddha	Schopenhauer
All desire leads to suffering	The world is "Will" — blind striving, never satisfied
Liberation comes through detachment	Liberation comes through denial of the Will
The self is an illusion	The world we experience is a projection — mere "representation"
Nirvana is not a paradise, but freedom from craving	Negating the Will brings peace, not death

Schopenhauer read deeply from Eastern texts, including the **Upanishads** and **Dhammapada**,
and declared:

> "Buddhism is the most excellent, the most rational, and the most noble religion the world has ever seen."
>
> He rejected the Christian idea of a creator-God,
> and replaced it with a vision of the universe as a **blind, purposeless will**,
> from which only inner renunciation—not external salvation—can set us free.

This is **pure philosophical Buddhism**, though expressed in the language of German idealism.

III. Spinoza: God as Nature, Self as Illusion

Baruch Spinoza, a 17th-century Dutch philosopher, was one of the most radical thinkers of the Enlightenment.
His core proposition: **God is not a person. God is Nature. God is the totality of existence.**

This idea resonates deeply with Buddhist principles of **non-theism**, **interdependence**, and **emptiness**.

Core Parallels:

Buddha	Spinoza
No creator God; all things arise from conditions	God is not a being, but the whole of Nature
All phenomena are interdependent	All modes are expressions of a single Substance
The self is not separate from the world	The individual is not independent from Nature
Enlightenment is seeing through illusion	Wisdom is the "intellectual love of God" (i.e. Nature)

Spinoza was excommunicated from his Jewish community for his "heresy."
He constructed a universe ruled not by divine judgment but by **mathematical harmony**,
and offered liberation not through faith but through understanding.

His "pantheism" is not a religion—it's **rational mysticism**, and its inner logic **mirrors the Buddha's vision of a non-self, interdependent reality.**

IV. Kant: Freedom, Reason, and the Inner Moral Law

Immanuel Kant may not have read Buddhist texts,
but his moral philosophy reflects **startling resonance** with the Buddha's Eightfold Path.

Kant believed:

- True freedom is not doing whatever you want,
but **acting from moral duty discovered through reason**.

- Goodness does not come from results or rewards,
but from **acting out of a sense of obligation**.

- We can never fully know the "thing-in-itself"; we live in a world of appearances.

Parallels to Buddhism:

Kant	**Buddha**
Freedom = Autonomy; reason governs will	Liberation = Mindfulness; Eightfold Path trains the mind
Moral action = acting from duty	Ethical behavior = arising from awareness and compassion
"Thing-in-itself" is unknowable	Reality is empty of fixed essence; all is impermanent
Moral law is within, not imposed from above	Precepts arise from insight, not external command

Kant's focus on **internal self-regulation** and **moral clarity** aligns with Buddhist ideas of **discipline and awareness**. Both reject **external salvation** in favor of **self-responsibility**.

V. Why Did They All Walk the Buddha's Path?

Despite their different contexts, all three philosophers came to a common realization:

> **Human suffering is not caused by the world alone, but by how we perceive, desire, and construct that world.**

They all sought to:

- **Deconstruct illusion** (no-self / representation / phenomenon);
- **Transcend desire** (detachment / will-denial / moral law);
- **Rebuild freedom** (nirvana / autonomy / oneness with Nature).

In this, they walked the same path as the Buddha.

They also **rejected**:

- A personal God;
- Reward-and-punishment systems;
- Religious authority as the source of meaning.

Each one proclaimed, in his own way, that **human beings must reclaim their lives through reason, clarity, and discipline—**
not through prayer, obedience, or miracles.

VI. Conclusion: A Silent Transmission Across Civilizations

To place the Buddha alongside Schopenhauer, Spinoza, and Kant
is not an exercise in cultural pride or comparison.

It is to recognize that:

> **The greatest thinkers of all civilizations have confronted the same riddle of being human.**
>
> The Buddha answered in silence and mindfulness.
> They answered in logic and ethics.
>
> But all rejected blind faith, all questioned the self, and all pointed inward.
>
> They did not ask: "Whom should I worship?"
> They asked:
>
> **"Am I truly thinking?
> Am I truly awake?"**

Chapter 5: Zhuangzi and Nietzsche

Twin Dissidents from Two Civilizations

I. Heretics from Different Worlds

In ancient Chinese culture, **Zhuangzi** was an outlier—someone who questioned fate, defied kings, and rejected Confucian moralism.
In Western philosophy, **Nietzsche** was a lone rebel—anti-religious, anti-morality, anti-system.

They were not system builders.
They were system destroyers.

They did not build temples.
They tore them down to reveal the sky.

Their mission was not to "construct truth" but to **shatter illusions**, allowing life to be seen in its most unfiltered form.

They never met, separated by 2,000 years and a continent.
And yet, their words often say the same thing:

- Opposition to anthropocentrism (human-centered worldview)
- Mockery of authority and conventional morality
- Celebration of individual freedom and spiritual liberation
- Rejection of fixed "truth"—embracing fluid, dynamic reality

II. Philosophical Structure: Zhuangzi vs. Nietzsche

Core Theme	Zhuangzi	Nietzsche
Truth	Truth is unspeakable; language is illusion	Truth is the will of power; no absolute truth exists
Authority	Satirizes kings, Confucians, and orthodox systems	Attacks God, the Church, and herd morality
Self and Ego	No fixed "self"; dissolves all distinctions	The self must be overcome and reborn through the "Übermensch"
Cosmos and Nature	Unity of all things; dreams and waking are indistinct	The world has no meaning; we create our own meanings
Way of Living	"Free wandering" (逍遥游); non-attachment, harmony	Tragic joy; embrace suffering and chaos as life's essence

III. Quote Atlas: Zhuangzi and Nietzsche Side-by-Side

Zhuangzi:

> "Why worry about where one is going? The body may be still like dead wood, and the heart may be like cold ashes."
> — *Zhuangzi, "The Secret of Caring for Life"*

Nietzsche:

> "A state of profound spiritual calmness, where the individual wills nothing."
> — *Thus Spoke Zarathustra*

Zhuangzi:

> "Everything transforms, and we cannot know the reason. This is called 'Heaven.'"
> — *Zhuangzi, "On Equalizing Things"*

Nietzsche:

> "Become who you are."
> — *Beyond Good and Evil*

These are not coincidences, but reflections of a **shared philosophical impulse**—to dissolve illusion, resist structure, and dance with the unknown.

IV. Their Philosophy Is Not a System — It's an Attitude

Zhuangzi's philosophy is not built on formal logic. It is a **way of seeing** the world:

- No judgment
- No clinging
- No binary between good and evil
- Dissolution of "self" into "all things"

Nietzsche's "Übermensch" is not a concrete ideal—it's a **mode of becoming**:

- The courage to deny
- The solitude to rebuild
- The strength to carry meaning after "God is dead"

Neither man sought to **define** the world.
They sought to **liberate** it.

They wrote with hammers.

Did the West Develop Nietzsche, While China Forgot Zhuangzi?

In China:

- Zhuangzi was absorbed into "Taoism," then trivialized as mystical folklore.
- After Confucian orthodoxy took over, Zhuangzi became a literary curiosity, not a living philosophy.
- There was no dialectic tradition—no open platform to debate, refine, and integrate his ideas.

In the West:

- Nietzsche's destruction gave birth to entire schools: Foucault, Derrida, existentialism, postmodernism.
- The West treats "rebels" as intellectual catalysts.
- Philosophy is allowed to oppose state ideology, creating a cycle of critique and renewal.

Nietzsche became a movement. Zhuangzi became a metaphor.

VI. Post-Philosophy: Beyond Systems, Toward Wisdom

Zhuangzi and Nietzsche are not philosophers of conclusion. They are philosophers of **disruption**.

They share a new kind of wisdom:

- **Not to define**, but to **experience**
- **Not to convert**, but to **unsettle**
- **Not to teach**, but to **deconstruct**

This connects them to Buddha, Heidegger, late Wittgenstein, and the roots of Zen:

> "True wisdom does not teach you what the world is.
> It shows you the limits of language and the emptiness of structure—
> And in that emptiness, freedom is born."

VII. Zhuangzi's Smile, Nietzsche's Laughter

Zhuangzi says:

> "The mushroom of the morning knows not the dusk.
> The summer insect knows not the winter."
> — So why expect humans to understand the universe?
>
> Nietzsche says:
>
> "He who has a why to live can bear almost any how."
> — Because we give meaning, not receive it.
>
> They both smiled—one softly, the other wildly.
> But behind both smiles was pain, and within that pain, truth.
>
> **Only when everything collapses, can true freedom begin.**

Chapter 6: Freud and Daoism

Where the Unconscious Meets Non-Action

I. Did Freud Discover the Unconscious — or Did the East Already Know?

In modern Western psychology, **Sigmund Freud** is hailed as the father of the unconscious.
He introduced a groundbreaking framework: repressed desires, childhood trauma, dream interpretation—together forming the foundation of **psychoanalysis**.

But if we look toward the East, we find that **Laozi and Zhuangzi** had already explored similar concepts.
They didn't use scientific language.
They used metaphors, paradoxes, and silence to express what lies beneath the surface of human consciousness.

Freud interpreted dreams.
Daoism asked:

> "Who knows when we are truly awake, and when we are dreaming?"
> — *Zhuangzi, "On Equalizing Things"*
>
> Both traditions used dreams to **challenge the structure of reality** and explore the inner workings of the mind.

II. Freud's Id, Ego, and Superego vs. Daoist Principles

Freud's structural model of the psyche consists of:

System	Freud's Definition	Daoist Parallel
Id (本我)	Primitive desires and instincts	"Dao follows nature" (道法自然)

Ego (自我)	Mediator between desires and reality	"Non-action" (无为)
Superego (超我)	Internalized morals, social rules, and guilt	Confucian codes, cultural "names" (名)

Freud advocated bringing the unconscious into consciousness—
To reclaim control of the self from repressed desires and overbearing norms.

Laozi said:

> "The highest virtue is like water. Water benefits all things and does not compete."
> — *Tao Te Ching*
>
> Water, in Daoism, symbolizes both the **Id** and the **Dao**—uncontrollable, flowing, nourishing, non-confrontational.

III. Therapy vs. Inner Awareness

Freud's Method:

- Free association
- Dream interpretation
- Analyzing childhood
- Goal: make the unconscious conscious

Daoist Practice:

- Stillness, breath, meditation
- Letting go of desire and judgment
- Embracing mystery, returning to "not knowing"
- Goal: dissolve the ego into nature

Dimension	Freud	Daoism
Methodology	Language, logic, analysis	Silence, observation, spontaneity
Objective	Self-mastery, psychic health	Non-self, inner peace
Main Conflict	Repression, cultural morality	Attachment, striving, name/fame
Ultimate Goal	Integrated self	Union with the Dao

IV. Is Freud a Western Daoist?

Surprisingly, we may ask:

Was Freud a "Western Laozi" in disguise?

- He rejected religion and morality → Like Zhuangzi mocking Confucians
- He traced behavior to inner drives → Like Daoists tracing action to "non-action"
- He sought to peel back masks → Like Laozi's "returning to the root"

Yes, Freud was more scientific, systematized, and grounded in medical methodology.
Daoism was more poetic, intuitive, and holistic.

But both tried to answer the same question:

Who am I? Why do I suffer? And how can I be free?

V. Why Did the West Create Psychology, While the East Remained with "Self-Cultivation"?

Key reasons include:

1. **Language structures**:
Western languages encourage logic and structure, suitable for building systems;
Eastern languages embrace ambiguity and metaphor, discouraging rigid codification.

2. **Cultural function of thought**:
In the West, philosophy confronts tradition;
In the East, it was co-opted to **maintain** social order (Confucianism).

3. **Institutional environments**:
The West had Renaissance, Enlightenment, and scientific revolutions;
China had centuries of centralized authoritarian rule that crushed heterodoxy.

So:

Freud became a discipline.
Zhuangzi became a quote.

VI. Future Paths: Merging Psychoanalysis and Eastern Wisdom

In today's world, anxiety, depression, and identity crises are widespread.
Pharmaceuticals dominate, yet healing often remains incomplete.

Meanwhile, Freud's framework alone is no longer enough.

We now see:

- **Mindfulness** emerging as a mainstream psychological tool
- Zen integrated into hospitals and universities
- Therapeutic models blending Freud, Jung, and Daoist thought
- Viktor Frankl, Carl Jung, and even Foucault drawing from Eastern philosophies

Mental health is not just about treating disorder.
It's about discovering who you are, and learning how to live.

VII. What Would Freud Learn in the East?

If Freud had read the *Tao Te Ching*, he might say:

> "The unconscious is not chaos—it is nature.
> And healing is not conquest, but surrender."
>
> And if Zhuangzi lived in today's psychoanalytic age,
> He might grin and whisper:
>
> "You call it therapy.
> I've always called it wandering free."

Chapter 7: From Religion to Philosophy to Politics

A Map of Civilizational Thought Evolution

I. The Three-Stage Evolution of Human Thought

Human civilizations tend to follow a three-stage trajectory in the evolution of thought:

1. **Religious Stage**
→ Social order is maintained through belief in gods, myths, and divine revelation.

2. **Philosophical Stage**
→ Rational inquiry replaces myth; thinkers begin asking about meaning, ethics, and existence.

3. **Political Stage**
→ Philosophical ideas are institutionalized as law, democracy, rights, and governance.

This evolution represents humanity's journey from "submission to divinity" to "self-governance through reason."

II. Comparative Civilizational Paths

Civilization	Religious Stage	Philosophical Stage	Political Stage
India	Brahmanism,	Upanishads, Nagarjuna's Middle Way	Gandhi's nonviolence, secular

	Hinduism, Buddhism		constitutionalis m
China	Confucian deification, Taoist mysticism	Laozi, Zhuangzi, Mohism, Chan Buddhism	Confucian imperial legitimacy, autocracy
Japan	Shinto-Buddhism synthesis	Zen, Nishida philosophy, Watsuji ethics	Meiji Constitution, parliamentary monarchy
Europe	Christianity (Catholicism)	Socratic inquiry, Kant, Nietzsche	Civil revolutions, human rights, democracy
Middle East	Islam	Avicenna, Averroes	Tensions between Islamic law and secular state

Only the Western tradition completes all three phases most structurally, while Eastern civilizations often stall at the **philosophy → politics** stage—particularly under authoritarian traditions.

III. Why Did China Fail to Institutionalize Philosophy?

1. **Confucianism as State Ideology**
→ Philosophy was absorbed into the imperial system, losing its critical edge.

2. **Civil Exam System Suppressed Innovation**
→ Rote memorization of classics replaced original thinking.

3. **Buddhism and Taoism Became Religious Folk Culture**
→ Deep philosophies were diluted into rituals, blessings, and spiritual protection.

4. **Political Repression of Heterodox Thought**
→ Schools like Mohism and Legalism were marginalized or erased.

Result:

China produced profound philosophy — but failed to translate it into modern institutions.

IV. Why Japan Succeeded in Entering Modernity

1. **Zen's Secularization and Rationality**
→ Zen promoted introspection, simplicity, and individual awakening.

2. **Synthesis with Western Thought**
→ Thinkers like Nishida Kitarō integrated Zen with Kant and Hegel.

3. **Meiji Reforms Established Constitutional Rule**
→ Balanced ceremonial monarchy with parliamentary governance.

4. **Postwar Constitution Separated Religion and State**
→ The emperor became symbolic; political power shifted to elected institutions.

V. Zhuangzi and Nietzsche: The Skeptics of Institutions

Thinker	Key Quote	Attitude Toward Politics
Zhuangzi	"Heaven and I were born together; all things and I are one."	The state is artificial; follow nature.
Nietzsche	"The state is the coldest of all cold monsters."	The state oppresses the soul; resist collective myths.

Despite centuries apart, both thinkers rejected systems that suppress individual spirit and autonomy.

VI. The Declining Role of Religion in Civil Society

Social Function	Religion's Response	Philosophy & Politics Alternative
Inner Consolation	Heaven, karma, divine protection	Existential thought, psychology, mindfulness
Social Order	Divine law, fate, obedience	Rule of law, civic education, equality
Support for the Weak	Charity, alms	Welfare systems, social safety nets
Moral Standards	Commandments, sacred texts, prohibitions	Humanist ethics, secular education

In modernity, **religion no longer serves as the sole source of meaning**—philosophy and politics now assume those roles.

VII. Toward a New Civilizational Path

1. **From Centralized Control to Decentralized Autonomy**

2. **From Obedience to Understanding**

3. **From Divine Rule to Rational Institutions**

4. **From Thought Suppression to Thought Flourishing**

5. **From Superstition to Reflective Consciousness**

Only by embracing this trajectory can China and East Asia **escape the dual trap of theocracy and authoritarianism**, and move toward a modern, pluralistic civilization.

Chapter 8: Why Chinese Philosophy Never Became a Political Institution

From Sagehood to State Tool: The Tragic Transition

I. The Gap Between Philosophy and Institutions in China

In the West, philosophy evolved into institutions:

→ Socrates inspired civic ethics

→ Aristotle classified regimes and civic virtues

→ Kant emphasized reason and moral law

→ Locke's ideas birthed constitutionalism

But in China, **philosophy was absorbed by power, not translated into institutional design**.

Despite its richness in ideal thought, Chinese philosophy failed to create systems of checks, rights, or democratic governance. Why?

II. Confucianism: From Ethics to Emperor Worship

1. **Confucius's benevolent politics became imperial dogma**
   - Originally an ethical ideal for ruling with virtue, Confucianism was co-opted by Han emperors into an ideology of absolute hierarchy.

2. **The "Three Bonds and Five Constants" systemized obedience**

- Ruler > subject, father > son, husband > wife — morality became a justification for authoritarian order.

3. **Anti-institutional bias**
   - Confucianism emphasized morality over law, virtue over structure, and human rule over legal rule.

📌 **Outcome**: Confucianism's critical thought was moralized, then politicized, and finally weaponized by the state.

III. Daoism and the Marginalization of Philosophical Freedom

1. **Zhuangzi rejected control, but lacked institutional design**
   - Deeply skeptical of artificial structures, Daoism encouraged detachment rather than reform.
2. **"Wuwei" (non-action) was co-opted by rulers**
   - Used as a cover for passive domination and state withdrawal from responsibility.
3. **Daoist philosophy devolved into mysticism**
   - Later Daoism shifted to alchemy, immortality, and ritual, abandoning rational philosophical inquiry.

IV. The Disappearance of Alternative Schools

1. **Mohism's logic and egalitarianism were erased**
   - Mozi championed universal love and anti-war thinking, but was purged from official history.

2. **Legalism became a tool of tyranny**
   - Han Feizi's ideas about law and order were adopted by the Qin but twisted into totalitarian surveillance and control.

☞ **Conclusion**: Philosophical schools with institutional potential were either eliminated or distorted.

V. How the Imperial Exam System Killed Philosophy

1. **What is tested becomes what is taught**
   - The civil service exam focused solely on Confucian classics, leaving no room for critical or alternative thought.

2. **Memorization over inquiry**
   - Students trained not to think, but to repeat.

3. **Thinking was repurposed to serve power**
   - Intellectual energy went into appeasing authority, not reforming it.

📌 China's educational system became a **filter of obedience**, not a platform for institutional imagination.

VI. How Buddhism Was De-Philosophized

1. **From reflection to superstition**
   - Buddhist insights into suffering and impermanence were turned into prayer rituals and magical thinking.

2. **Zen's brief brilliance faded**
   - Early Chan/Zen Buddhism promoted awareness and introspection, but later became rigid and guru-centered.

3. **No integration into law or governance**
   - Profound ideas like "no-self" or "dependent origination" were never translated into social contracts or constitutions.

VII. Four Cultural Roots of China's Institutional Failure

Factor	Description
Cultural Insularity	The Sinocentric worldview rejected outside ideas and innovations.
Hierarchical Mentality	Deep-rooted class and status systems made equality seem unnatural.
Worship of Authority	The triad of ruler-father-teacher made critical thought sacrilegious.
Pragmatic Materialism	Philosophy was seen as "useless," resulting in short-term power tactics.

VIII. What Is Needed for Philosophical Institutionalization?

A philosophy capable of shaping institutions must contain:

- **Universal principles** – dignity, justice, limits to power
- **Translatable pathways** – from thought to legislation
- **Public participation** – philosophy becomes collective consciousness
- **Capacity for self-correction** – built-in critique and reform mechanisms

📌 Western modernity succeeded not because its philosophy was better, but because it became **institutionalized**.

IX. A Possible Path Forward: Five Philosophical Reforms

1. **De-mystify philosophy** – Return to rational ethics and social inquiry
2. **Reform education** – From indoctrination to reflective dialogue
3. **Infuse politics with Eastern ideas** – Suffering, impermanence, mutual care
4. **Write philosophy into constitutions** – Make dignity and mindfulness legal foundations
5. **Study Japan, Germany, Taiwan** – Learn how others rebuilt post- authoritarian societies

Chapter 9: Buddha and Marx: Misunderstood Idealists of Social Liberation

From Compassion and Equality to Authoritarian Appropriation

I. A Common Starting Point: Radical Concern for Suffering and Injustice

- **Buddha**: Born a prince, renounced privilege, and turned his attention to the root of human suffering, articulating the Four Noble Truths and the path to liberation through inner transformation and compassion.

- **Marx**: Born into the bourgeois class, turned against capitalism after observing the exploitation of workers, proposing historical materialism and revolution toward a classless society.

Despite vast differences in time, culture, and method, both thinkers shared a **fundamental concern with injustice, suffering, and inequality**:

Comparison	Buddha	Marx
Core Concern	Suffering from attachment and ego	Exploitation under capitalist systems
Philosophical Base	Emptiness (śūnyatā), impermanence, no-self	Historical materialism, class struggle
Ultimate Ideal	Liberation (nirvana), universal compassion	Classless society, collective freedom

II. Shared Critique of Ownership and Possession

- **Buddha** saw attachment to "self" and "possessions" as the roots of suffering.

- **Marx** saw **private property** as the engine of social inequality and class oppression.

Both questioned the **legitimacy of ownership as a source of meaning or power**, though with different methods:

- Buddha promoted **inner liberation**, through awareness and detachment.
- Marx advocated **external revolution**, through struggle and structural change.

III. From Philosophy to Dogma: How Both Were Misused

Buddha's teachings → Turned into religion:

- Originally a **path of introspection and wisdom**, it was later transformed into a system of worship, ritual, and superstition.

- Averse to deities and idols, Buddhism eventually evolved into temples, prayer rituals, and "blessings for wealth and children."

- **Zen** Buddhism revived the spirit of inquiry for a time, but later succumbed to institutional rigidity.

Marx's theory → Turned into ideology:

- Originally a **critique of capitalism and a vision for worker liberation**, it became dogma in Leninist-Stalinist regimes.

- "Dictatorship of the proletariat" replaced **collective freedom** with centralized authoritarianism.

- Marx's critical method became a **state religion**, unchallengeable and absolute.

📌 **In both cases**, ideas meant to **liberate people** were **transformed into tools of control**.

III. Middle Way vs. Revolutionary Struggle

Philosophical Mode	Buddha: The Middle Way	Marx: Dialectical Struggle
Worldview	Plural, fluid, impermanent	Dualistic: oppressor vs. oppressed
Method	Observation, moderation, detachment	Negation, conflict, overthrow
Goal	Inner peace, end of suffering	Structural equality, end of exploitation

Buddha emphasized **awareness and internal transformation**, while Marx focused on **external systems and power dynamics**.

They can complement each other — but have often been **mistaken as opposites**.

IV. Institutional Designs: Who Aligns More with Modern Civilization?

Metric	**Buddha's Philosophy**	**Marxist Theory**
Respect for Individual Freedom	✅ Rooted in no-self, non-domination	⚠️ Often subordinated to collective vision
Violence Inclination	❌ Advocates non-violence	⚠️ Revolution often co-opted by violent regimes
Religious Tendencies	✅ Encourages personal belief and compassion	❌ Turned into dogmatic ideology
System Design Potential	❌ Lacks institutional roadmap	✅ Proposes structural transformation

Both contain valuable elements, but **neither** in its original form provides a **complete modern democratic framework**.

VI. A New Synthesis: Can Buddha and Marx Be Reunited?

A new civilization might build on both:

1. **Buddha's mindful compassion × Marx's social analysis**
→ See systemic injustice clearly, but act with care and consciousness.

2. **Use the Middle Way in political transitions**
→ Avoid extremes: neither authoritarian equality nor unfettered capitalism.

3. **Institutionalize compassion**
→ Build systems that protect the weak, without removing agency.

4. **Desacralize both traditions**
→ Make philosophy practical again — neither mystical religion nor rigid ideology.

VII. A Warning: Philosophy Turned Into Political Tools

- **Buddha's "compassion"** can become an opiate to pacify citizens under unjust conditions.
- **Marx's "class struggle"** can become justification for endless purges and centralized repression.
- **Without mindfulness and critical thinking**, both become **mirrors of the very suffering they sought to end**.

VIII. Conclusion: They Meant to Liberate — But Were Used to Enslave

Thinker	Original Purpose	Misused Outcome
Buddha	Enlightenment, detachment, peace	Ritualism, magical thinking, obedience
Marx	Liberation, justice, equality	Authoritarianism, thought control

📌 To return to true philosophy, we must **reinterpret** what they **really meant**, not what regimes turned them into.

Chapter 10: Zen, Kant, and the Awakening of Human Rights

From Inner Moral Law to the Ethical Foundation of Modern Institutions

I. How Is Kant's "Moral Law" Different from Buddhist "Precepts"?

- Kant famously wrote:
  "Two things fill the mind with ever new and increasing admiration and awe… the starry heavens above and the moral law within."

- For Kant, morality was not dictated from outside, but derived from reason itself.

- Early Buddhist precepts (sīla), like the Five Precepts or the Bodhisattva vows, were also **meant to be self-imposed**, not externally enforced.

📌 But over time, **Buddhism was turned into belief**, while Kant pushed **self-reasoned ethics** to the philosophical frontier.

Comparison	Buddhist Precepts (Early)	Kant's Moral Law
Source	Insight into suffering and impermanence	Reason and universality
Form	Concrete behavioral guidelines	"Act only on maxims you can will to be universal law"

Purpose	Liberation from suffering	Respect for every individual as an end in themselves
Divine Origin?	No	No

II. Zen Buddhism: Eastern Practice of Moral Autonomy

- Zen (Chan) emphasized **sudden insight**, not scriptures or rituals.

- From *The Platform Sutra*: "The Buddha is not in the temple, but in the heart."
- Zen's "gateless gate" is really a **pathway to inner judgment and freedom**.

📌 In this sense, **Zen mirrors Kant** — both champion **autonomy**, though from different traditions: one spiritual, one rational.

III. Human Rights: From Submission to Sovereignty

- In feudal China, "fate" was fixed and "virtue" meant obedience.
- Kant reversed the paradigm:
"Man is not a means but an end."
- His philosophy directly influenced:
    - The **Declaration of the Rights of Man**
    - Modern constitutions
    - The **UN Charter**

Feudal Ideals	Kantian Ideals
Submit to Heaven	Question authority
Hierarchical ethics	Rational self-legislation
Father–Son–Ruler	Every person is autonomous and dignified

III. Why Japan Absorbed Kant Earlier Than China

- After the Meiji Restoration, Japan actively translated Kant, Hegel, Rousseau.
- Zen Buddhism had already cultivated **self-discipline and introspection**.
- Though Japan did not fully realize liberal democracy, Kant's ideals shaped:
    - Education
    - Ethical discourse
    - Early legal reform

📌 In contrast, late Qing China was still trapped in:

- Emperor worship
- Moral hierarchy
- Exam-based memorization systems

V. What If Buddha Had Met Kant?

Imagine if Buddhism had **not become deified**, and had instead dialogued with Kant's rational ethics:

Fusion Hypothesis	Potential Outcome

Precepts become philosophical ethics	From superstition to rational virtue
Nirvana redefined as human dignity	Not just escape, but fulfillment of human value
"All beings suffer" becomes "All deserve dignity"	Compassion evolves into legal protection for rights

📌 Not just **Compassion (Karuna)**, but **Justice**.

VI. A Triangular Foundation for Institutions:

Buddha × Zen × Kant

Modern institutions are not just systems — they are **ethical machines**.

They require:

1. **Respect for all people** (Buddha's compassion)
2. **Self-governing discipline** (Zen's awareness)
3. **Rational structure and critique** (Kant's universality)

📌 Institutions must embody both **spiritual warmth** and **logical scaffolding**.

VII. What East Asia Still Lacks Today

Social Ills	Missing Philosophical Root
Power without accountability	Kant's legal rationality + moral duty
Social coldness and egoism	Buddha's compassion and no-self teaching
Thought control, education as obedience	Zen's insight and non-dual thinking

Lack of protection for the weak	Human rights: all persons as ends

VIII. Toward a Rehumanized Philosophy

We don't need **philosopher-idols** anymore. We need:

- **Kant who walks**: Rational ethics as public governance
- **Buddha without incense**: Awakening, not worship
- **Zen master in jeans**: Modern awareness, not mysticism

📌 Philosophy must move from **temples and books** to **streets and constitutions**.

Chapter 11: Zhuangzi and Nietzsche: The Spirit of Rebellion

From the "Usefulness of Uselessness" to the Ultimate Pursuit of Freedom

1. Zhuangzi's Rebellion: The Philosophy of "Uselessness"

Zhuangzi once said:

> "The usefulness of what is useless is the greatest use of all."
>
> In the Warring States era, when most philosophers were debating how to govern the state, how to strengthen the army, and how to serve the ruler, Zhuangzi took a radically different path:

- He rejected politics and utility;
- He pursued **freedom of the spirit and detachment from the world**;
- He championed a **life of wandering, spontaneity, and self-liberation**.

📌 In a society dominated by hierarchy, Confucian ritual, and state control, Zhuangzi's philosophy was a bold **exit from power**—a form of **intellectual civil disobedience**.

2. Nietzsche's Übermensch: The Western Echo of Zhuangzi

Nietzsche proclaimed:

> "God is dead. Now we must become gods ourselves."
>
> This was not mere atheism—it was a radical rejection of imposed morality:

- Why should we obey inherited values?
- Who defines what is "good" or "evil"?
- Why is obedience a virtue, and not creativity?

In this rebellion, Nietzsche deeply echoes Zhuangzi:

Dimension	**Zhuangzi**	**Nietzsche**
Authority	Satirized rulers and state orthodoxy	Attacked God, Church, moral norms
Goal	Spiritual wandering, inner freedom	Übermensch, radical self-creation
Methodology	Allegories, dreams, paradoxes	Aphorisms, polemics, poetic fury
Value Critique	Critique of usefulness and control	Revaluation of all values

📌 If Zhuangzi stood for "non-action and liberation" in the East, Nietzsche was the "creator through destruction" in the West.

3. The Shared Essence of Rebellion: Awakening of the Individual

Despite time and culture differences, both Zhuangzi and Nietzsche voiced a singular truth:

> The individual must awaken, resist external authority, and reclaim the self.
>
> Their rebellions were not anarchic chaos—but philosophical awakening:
>
> - Zhuangzi reminded us we are not mere citizens or servants—we are **beings between Heaven and Earth**;
> - Nietzsche challenged us to abandon blind belief—we are **our own creators**.

4. Why Did the East Not Follow Zhuangzi?

Zhuangzi's philosophy had the potential to lead China into a civilization of inner freedom and intellectual emancipation. Yet history chose another route. Why?

1. **Confucian Domination**: After the Han dynasty's embrace of Confucian orthodoxy, Zhuangzi was sidelined.
2. **Imperial Utility**: Zhuangzi's ideas were too destabilizing for centralized authority.
3. **Esoteric Style**: His dream-like, allegorical writing, though poetic, lacked institutional impact.

4. **Lack of Social Response**: China had no equivalent of the Enlightenment or democratic revolution.

📌 Zhuangzi remained in literature, not law—in ink, not in institutions.

5. Why Did the West Ultimately Embrace Nietzsche?

Though marginalized during his life, Nietzsche was rediscovered after World War II:

- He became a pillar of postmodern thought and "deconstruction of power."
- Psychologists embraced his insights into human desire and repression.
- Philosophers recognized him as a turning point after Kant and Hegel.

📌 The pluralism of Western systems allowed Nietzsche's rebellion to survive, evolve, and influence the structure itself.

6. From Rebellion to Structure: What Comes Next?

Rebellion is only the beginning of awakening—not its end.

- Zhuangzi and Nietzsche **awakened the self**;
- But we must now **design systems that protect that self**.

Element	Path to Realization
Individual Awakening	Education, critical reading, pluralism
Free Thinking	Freedom of speech, decentralized media
Tolerant Institutions	Constitutional protections, human rights
Religion ≠ Philosophy	End theological dominance of reason

📌 Their spirit must live not only in ideas—but in **laws, norms, and systems** that nurture individuality and protect dissent.

7. Epilogue: Beyond Usefulness—Toward the Century of Being

We still live in an age ruled by utility:

- Education must be "practical";
- People must be "productive";
- Thinking must be "correct";
- Philosophy must be "functional."

Yet Zhuangzi and Nietzsche whisper otherwise:

True freedom is to exist **without needing to prove your worth**.

Like the wind, light, dreams, poetry, love...
They may seem "useless," yet they form the essence of human dignity.

📌 Without these "useless" things, civilization becomes a machine—efficient, but lifeless.

Chapter 12: Philosophy Hijacked by Politics

Why Are Philosophers Feared by Kings and Praised by Tyrants

Only After They're Dead?

I. Why Is Philosophy So Dangerous?

Throughout history, philosophy has never been just abstract theory—it has always meant one thing:

The courage to question the structure of power.

And that is exactly what every authority fears.

Philosophy asks, "What is justice?"
Power says, "Whatever I say it is."

From Socrates to Confucius, from Spinoza to Rousseau, philosophers have been silenced, exiled, imprisoned, or condemned.

Philosopher	What Happened to Them
Socrates	Sentenced to death by democratic Athens
Zhu Xi	Attacked by officials as "heresy"
Spinoza	Excommunicated by his religious community
Lu Xun	Mocked as a "mad dog," silenced by society

📌 The problem is never that philosophy is dangerous.
It's that it exposes **how fragile the illusion of power really is.**

II. From Doctrine to Party Lines: When Philosophy Becomes a Tool

The greatest irony is this:

> The same systems that silenced thinkers while they lived
> often worship them once they're dead—
> only after **editing their words and castrating their message.**

- Confucius was transformed into a tool of monarchy, though he championed virtue over birth.

- The Buddha's teachings of liberation became masked in temples and incense.

- Marx's critique of capitalism was weaponized by Lenin and Stalin into a totalitarian state.

Philosophy becomes a **decoration** for regimes—no longer a tool for thinking, but a tool for control.

III. Why Are Philosophers Celebrated Only After They Die?

Because **living philosophers ask dangerous questions**.

Dead philosophers can be quoted selectively.

- Plato's *Republic* is reduced to the idea of the "philosopher king"—ignoring his critiques of power.

- Zhuangzi is painted as a "quiet recluse"—ignoring his subversive view of authority.

- Nietzsche is misused by Nazis for "Übermensch" rhetoric—ignoring his hatred for nationalism and herd morality.

📌 **Cut-and-paste philosophy is a silent assassination of the original thinker.**

IV. What Real Philosophy Must Do Now

To truly reclaim philosophy, we must **de-sanctify** it:

Trap	What It Does	Remedy
Dogma	Freezes thought into rigid belief systems	Return to open-ended questioning
Idol Worship	Turns philosophers into saints, not teachers	Read their full work, not quotes
Political Co-option	Uses philosophy as power's mask	Reconnect with the human soul beneath it

> **Philosophy is not for the throne.**
> **It is for the street, the kitchen, the classroom, the soul.**

Final Reflection

> "The one who tells you *not to think* is the one most afraid you will wake up."
>
> That is the essence of power—and the mission of real philosophy is to break that spell.

Chapter 13: Reclaiming Wisdom: Stop Worshipping, Start Awakening

The Buddha was never a god. He was a philosopher.

I. Philosophy Dressed in Gold: Religion Betrays the Buddha

If the Buddha were alive today, he would likely be the **first to question** the very temples that claim his legacy.

All of it:

- The "donation pools" for merit accumulation,
- The chanting rituals treated like magical incantations,
- The worship of statues for safety and fortune,
- The monks idolized as spiritual CEOs,
- The commercialized "Dharma talks," paid blessings, feng shui rituals...

These have little to do with his teachings of:

- **No-self (anatta)**
- **Impermanence (anicca)**
- **Liberation through wisdom—not faith**

📌 **The Buddha was not a deity, nor a saint, nor a bringer of fortune.**

He was a human being who understood suffering—and showed a path out of it.

II. The Deepest Betrayal: Selling Illusions in the Name of Liberation

The true betrayal of Buddhism today lies in turning wisdom into superstition, and inner clarity into external ritual.

False Dharma Narrative	Hidden Logic Behind It
"Chant this mantra 10,000 times to change your life"	Mechanical repetition replaces insight
"Worship this statue for protection"	Material objects replace inner strength
"Listen to masters and you'll be enlightened"	Outsourcing truth, abandoning self-effort
"Obey the Sangha without question"	Killing the root of free inquiry
"Buy blessings, earn merit"	Karma becomes a transaction, not awareness

📌 **This is not Buddhism. This is mental manipulation packaged in spirituality.**
It is spiritual consumerism—designed to soothe, not to awaken.

III. From Worship to Questioning

We must **stop worshipping** if we are to start **waking up**.

- The worshipper mimics words.
- The seeker examines their truth.
- The believer wants miracles.

- The awakened faces reality.
- The faithful flee suffering.
- The wise turn toward it and transform it.

The Buddha did not fear questions.
But many modern "masters" fear nothing more than your critical mind.

📌 **Why? Because if you think for yourself, you don't need them.**

IV. Awakening Is Not Believing. It Is Seeing Clearly.

Real awakening is not in rituals, robes, or incense.
It is in daring to see through illusion.

- When you no longer need a Buddha statue — you're closer to the Buddha.

- When you no longer rely on a guru — your path truly begins.

- When you stop believing blindly — wisdom enters.

Awakening begins when you ask:

"Am I truly facing my pain?"
"Am I aware of my own fear, greed, and delusion?"
"Can I observe my life directly, without excuse, ritual, or dependency?"

This is not Buddhist dogma.
This is universal human freedom — grounded in awareness, not authority.

V. The Future: Philosophy for All, Wisdom Within

Tomorrow's civilization must not be built on religious obedience or political doctrine,
but on **mass philosophical literacy and collective inner awareness**.

Past	Future
Buddha = object of worship	Buddha = philosopher, model of inquiry
Buddhism = institutional religion	Dharma = personal path of awareness
Temple = sacred space	Daily life = field of practice
"Rely on others"	"Be a lamp unto yourself"
Enlightenment = elite goal	Wisdom = basic human right and duty

A truly awakened society would look like this:

- People don't "believe" blindly — they understand.
- People don't "follow" blindly — they observe.
- People don't "pray for escape" — they cultivate resilience.

Awakening is not magic. It's the clearest realism.
Not transcendence — but presence.

Conclusion: Wisdom is the Highest Compassion

True philosophy is not cold logic. It is the clearest light of humanity.

I. Philosophy is Not an Academic Game—It's a Guide in Times of Collapse

Today's world faces three simultaneous collapses:

- **Economic Collapse**: Wealth concentrates while the majority are stripped of basic rights.
- **Political Collapse**: Power spins out of control, truth disappears, people lose their voice.
- **Spiritual Collapse**: Faith becomes a commodity, philosophy is pushed aside, and the soul is hollowed out.

In such a world, what we need is not **more belief**, but **more thinking, more awakening, more becoming truly human**.

And that begins by:

📌 **Returning philosophy to daily life, and rescuing wisdom from the altar.**

II. The Buddha's Real Compassion Was to Help People Wake Up

What made the Buddha great was not that he could bless you, protect you, or perform miracles.

It was this:

- He revealed that the root of suffering is **ignorance**.
- He taught that the path to liberation is **wisdom**.
- He insisted that true awakening must be **walked step by step** by the individual.

He never said, "Believe in me and you will be saved."

He only said, **"Be a lamp unto yourself."**

But today?

- **Buddha has been commercialized, his teachings turned into performance, his practice into product.**
- **Suffering is no longer examined—it's "cleansed." Truth is no longer sought—it's "blessed."**

This is the deepest betrayal of his wisdom.
And the grandest illusion of our age.

III. From Philosophy, We Build Real Compassion

Real compassion is not helping people escape pain.
It's helping them understand it.

Real compassion is not "Let me save you."
It's "You have the power to save yourself."

Real compassion gives people the strength to face reality, not comforting lies to escape it.

Philosophy's power lies not in giving answers,
but in giving people back the right to ask.

In an age where everyone is looking for quick relief,
we must declare:

📌 **To think is to care. To doubt is to wake.
Wisdom is the highest form of love.**

IV. A Letter to the Future: Don't Believe — Awaken

This book is not asking you to become a "follower of Buddha."
Nor to worship any "great philosopher."

It is asking:

- **Who are you, really?**
- **Do you truly see yourself?**
- **Are you living a free, conscious, self-responsible life?**

The civilization of tomorrow cannot be built on religion, ideology, or capital.
It must be built on **awakened individuals with dignity and depth.**

V. Are You Ready?

If the Buddha stood before you today,
He would not say, "Worship me."
He would ask, "Are you ready to face the truth?"

If Nietzsche were alive today,
He would not say, "Follow me."

He would say, "Destroy the idols that enslave your mind."

If Zhuangzi awoke in this era,
He would not say, "This is the Way."
He would ask, "Have you begun your own journey of freedom?"

This Book is Not an End. It's a Beginning.

May you close this book not as a **believer**,
but as a human being who reclaims:

- Your clarity,
- Your agency,
- Your ability to think, doubt, and awaken.

Do not believe in the Buddha—become your own Buddha.
Do not quote philosophy—live your own philosophy.
Do not flee reality—pierce through it, and find your freedom.

Afterword: When Worship Ends, Awakening Begins

This book was never meant to give you answers.

It was written to **burn down the false altars**—
And **plant a single seed of fire** in your mind.

A fire that says: **Do not bow. Do not follow. Begin.**

This is not a book of belief.
It is a book of **un-belief**, of **disillusionment**, of **awakening**.

It is not the conclusion of a journey.
It is the invitation to begin your own.

⛩ The Buddha Did Not Build Temples—He Tore Down Illusions

The Buddha never asked for worship.
He never asked for incense, chants, robes, or temples.

What he taught was:

- **Impermanence** — What you cling to will pass.
- **No-Self** — What you think you are is not what you are.
- **Interdependence** — Your suffering is not fate, it's cause and effect.

Yet what did we do?

We turned him into

a **spiritual brand**,
a **commercial idol**,
a **lucky charm**,
a **dealer of comfort** in a collapsing world.

> We misunderstood his silence as permission to build an empire of noise.

⚖ The West Did Not Worship the Buddha — But Some Understood Him

Schopenhauer. Spinoza. Kant. Nietzsche.

They never called themselves Buddhists.
But in their own language—through doubt, critique, and deep reason—
they touched the same truths.

They walked the path **from reason to emptiness**,
from **ego to awareness**,
from **control to surrender**.

And what of the East?

Still trapped in rituals.
Still selling incense.
Still preaching escape.
Still fearing thought.

This is not a shame to hide.
It is the **point of awakening**.

🧭 Philosophy is Not Cold Logic — It is the Deepest Compassion

In an age of collapsing systems and rising despair,
philosophy is not a luxury. It is a necessity.

Real compassion is not "saving" others.
It is **giving them the tools to see clearly**.

Real compassion is not saying "You will be okay."
It is saying, "**You have the strength to face what's not okay.**"
In this time of crisis, we must stop asking:

- **Who can save us?**

And start asking:

- **Who can still think? Who dares to awaken?**

A Message to the Future: Do Not Worship—Awaken

When you close this book:

- **Do not praise the Buddha.** Become one.
- **Do not quote the philosophers.** Think like one.
- **Do not search for truth.** Live as if truth matters.

If this book made you stop and think—
Even once.
Even for one breath.

Then its purpose is complete.

May you carry the flame of thought in an age of darkness.
May you question, not to destroy, but to illuminate.
May you never bow blindly, and never forget: you were born to wake.

Appendix A: Comparative Table – Buddha vs. Schopenhauer / Spinoza / Kant

Theme	Buddha (Siddhartha Gautama)	Schopenhauer	Spinoza	Kant
Core Philosophy	Suffering arises from desire; liberation through detachment	Will is the root of suffering; salvation through negation of will	All is one substance (God/Nature); rejects dualism	Moral law arises from reason; duty has primacy over desire
View of the Self	"No-self" (Anatta) — self is illusion	Self is driven by irrational will	Self is part of divine substance	Self is bound by categorical imperative
Goal of Life	Enlightenment (Nirvana): cessation of craving	Escape from will through ascetic contemplation	Joy through intellectual love of God/Nature	Moral action from rational duty, not desire
View of Desire	Root of suffering — must be overcome	Irrational, endless pain	Natural but must be governed by reason	Resisted if against moral law

Metaphysical Stance	Non-theistic; impermanence; interdependence	Pessimistic idealism	Pantheistic rationalism	Critical idealism; “thing-in-itself” unknowable
Method of Liberation	Meditation, mindfulness, ethical practice	Aesthetic contemplation; will-denial	Rational understanding; intellectual love of Nature	Practical reason, autonomy, moral action
Relation to Religion	Rejects ritual and deities; path of wisdom	Religion as illusion	Redefines God as Nature	Rational faith within limits of reason

🔎 **Insight**: All four thinkers emphasize *inner transformation, rational detachment, and ethical or contemplative practice over external salvation or ritual.*

Appendix B: Quote Atlas – Zhuangzi vs. Nietzsche

Theme	Zhuangzi (Chuang Tzu)	Friedrich Nietzsche
On Truth & Language	"The fish trap exists because of the fish; once you've caught the fish, you can forget the trap."	"All language is metaphor. Truths are illusions we have forgotten are illusions."
On Identity & Change	"Am I Zhuangzi who dreamed he was a butterfly, or a butterfly dreaming he is Zhuangzi?"	"You must become who you are."
On Morality	"Right and wrong are like day and night — who can fix their boundaries?"	"Good and evil are not eternal; man created them."
On Authority	"The greatest thief is the one who wears the emperor's robe."	"God is dead. And we have killed him."
On Freedom	"The perfect man has no self; the divine man takes no credit."	"The Übermensch creates his own values."
On Nature	"Heaven and Earth are one with me; the ten thousand things and I are one."	"Live in accordance with nature: not as slave, but as creator."

🔎 **Insight**: Zhuangzi dissolves boundaries through paradox; Nietzsche shatters them through confrontation. Both liberate the individual from imposed truths.

Appendix C: Timeline – Zen Buddhism & Japan's Intellectual Modernization

Period	Key Event / Evolution	Impact on Japanese Thought
538 CE	Buddhism introduced from China via Korea	Early Mahayana influence; temples established
8th Century	Rise of Tendai & Shingon schools	Mystical ritual, imperial patronage
12th Century	Zen (Rinzai & Soto) introduced from China	Focus on meditation, inner realization
13th–14th Century	Kamakura period: Zen adopted by samurai	Bushidō ethic infused with Zen discipline and detachment
16th–17th Century	Tea ceremony, Ikebana, Noh shaped by Zen aesthetics	Everyday life as philosophical practice
1868	Meiji Restoration	Zen as cultural resilience amid Westernization
20th Century	D.T. Suzuki and others spread Zen to the West	Zen as a bridge between Eastern and Western thought

🔎 **Insight**: Japan transformed Buddhism from a belief system into a *living practice*. Zen became philosophy in action, not dogma.

Appendix D: Essential Readings

🕉 Buddha & Early Buddhism

- **Primary**: *Dhammapada, Majjhima Nikāya, Samyutta Nikāya*
- **Secondary**:
- Walpola Rahula, *What the Buddha Taught*
- Bhikkhu Bodhi (ed.), *In the Buddha's Words*

🐟 Zhuangzi

- **Primary**: *Zhuangzi* (Inner Chapters)
- **Translations**:
- Burton Watson, *The Complete Works of Chuang Tzu*
- A.C. Graham, *Chuang Tzu: The Inner Chapters*

⚔ Nietzsche

- **Primary**: *Thus Spoke Zarathustra, Beyond Good and Evil, The Gay Science*
- **Commentary**:
- Walter Kaufmann, *Nietzsche: Philosopher, Psychologist, Antichrist*
- Graham Parkes (ed.), *Nietzsche and Asian Thought*

🧠 Freud

- **Primary**: *The Interpretation of Dreams, Civilization and Its Discontents*
- **Comparative**:
- Jerry Piven, *The Tao of Freud*
- Axel Hoffer, *Freud and the Buddha*

🧭 Kant / Spinoza / Schopenhauer

- **Primary**:
- Kant: *Critique of Pure Reason, Groundwork for the Metaphysics of Morals*
- Spinoza: *Ethics*
- Schopenhauer: *The World as Will and Representation*
- **Comparative**:
- U. App, *Schopenhauer and Buddhism*
- A. Deleuze, *The Hidden Connections: Spinoza and Eastern Thought*

Appendix E: Map of Philosophical Evolution Across Civilizations

Conceptual Flow (can be visualized as diagram):

[Spiritual Intuition]
↓
[Mythology]
↓
[Religion] → (Dogma / Ritual / Power)
↓
[Philosophy] → (Critical Thought / Self-Inquiry / Ethics)
↓
[Politics] → (Ideologies / Systems / Control)
↓
[Rebirth?] → (Return to Wisdom? Integration? Or Collapse?)

Civilizational Paths

Civilization	Religion Dominant?	Did Philosophy Survive?	Political Integration	Notes
India	Yes (Hinduism, Buddhism)	Partially (absorbed into theology)	Caste-based states	Philosophy subsumed into theology

China	Yes (Confucianism as civil religion)	Suppressed after Han	Strong imperial system	Daoism & Buddhism turned mystical
Japan	Yes, but Zen secularized	Yes (Zen as practice)	Moderately integrated	Zen fused with modernization
Europe	Yes (Christianity)	Revived in Enlightenment	Church → State secularism	Tension between reason and faith
Islamic World	Yes (Islam)	Yes (Golden Age, then suppressed)	Theocratic alignment	Ibn Sina, Al-Farabi marginalized
Modern West	No (Post-religious)	Yes (diverse schools)	Shaped democracy	Risk: Philosophy commodified

🔎 **Insight**: Civilizations thrive when philosophy emancipates from religion, and decline when politics absorbs both.

www.ingramcontent.com/pod-product-compliance
Lightning Source LLC
LaVergne TN
LVHW010630100826
845148LV00014B/3177

* 9 7 9 8 9 0 2 1 7 0 2 2 8 *